Japan

Tradition, Culture, and Daily Life

MAJOR NATIONS IN A GLOBAL WORLD

Books in the Series

Japan

Tradition, Culture, and Daily Life

MAJOR NATIONS IN A GLOBAL WORLD

Michael Centore

Mason Crest

Mason Crest
450 Parkway Drive, Suite D
Broomall, PA 19008
www.masoncrest.com

Printed and bound in the United States of America.

First printing
9 8 7 6 5 4 3 2 1

Series ISBN: 978-1-4222-3339-9
ISBN: 978-1-4222-3347-4
ebook ISBN: 978-1-4222-8587-9

The Library of Congress has cataloged the hardcopy format(s) as follows:

Library of Congress Cataloging-in-Publication Data

Centore, Michael, 1980-
  Japan / by Michael Centore.
    pages cm. -- (Major nations in a global world: tradition, culture, and daily life)
  Includes index.

  ISBN 978-1-4222-3347-4 (hardback) -- ISBN 978-1-4222-3339-9 (series) -- ISBN 978-1-4222-8587-9 (ebook)
  1. Japan--Juvenile literature. 2. Japan--Social life and customs--Juvenile literature. 3. Japan--Civilization--Juvenile literature. I. Title.
  DS806.C43 2015
  952--dc23
                          2015005031

Developed and produced by MTM Publishing, Inc.
        Project Director   Valerie Tomaselli
        Copyeditor   Lee Motteler/Geomap Corp.
        Editorial Coordinator Andrea St. Aubin

Indexing Services   Andrea Baron, Shearwater Indexing

Art direction and design by Sherry Williams, Oxygen Design Group

Contents

KEY ICONS TO LOOK FOR:

Words to Understand: These words with their easy-to-understand definitions will increase the reader's understanding of the text, while building vocabulary skills.

Sidebars: This boxed material within the main text allows readers to build knowledge, gain insights, explore possibilities, and broaden their perspectives by weaving together additional information to provide realistic and holistic perspectives.

Research Projects: Readers are pointed toward areas of further inquiry connected to each chapter. Suggestions are provided for projects that encourage deeper research and analysis.

Text-Dependent Questions: These questions send the reader back to the text for more careful attention to the evidence presented there.

Series Glossary of Key Terms: This back-of-the book glossary contains terminology used throughout this series. Words found here increase the reader's ability to read and comprehend higher-level books and articles in this field.

The Imperial Palace in the Chiyoda district of Tokyo.

MAJOR NATIONS IN A GLOBAL WORLD: JAPAN

INTRODUCTION

As an island group situated on the western margin of the Pacific Ocean, Japan is quite literally a place apart. Though its urban centers are some of the fastest-paced, most technologically connected areas on the planet, Japanese culture values patience, serenity, and a sense of balance in all things. These virtues are apparent in the day-to-day activities of the people as much as in artistic or religious forms of expression. Something as simple as brewing a pot of tea or preparing a meal can become an aesthetic experience.

Japan's history of the samurai warrior and the code of honor have helped instill a sense of duty to one's country. This carries beyond political and diplomatic life and influences family dynamics. Faithfulness to one's elders is an important quality. There are also many unwritten rules that help guide social interactions outside of the family. This rootedness in age-old traditions coupled with an ability to think in new and innovative ways is what makes Japan such a respected presence throughout the world.

The physical landscape of Japan also shapes its national character. The rhythm of the sea, the changeless faces of its mountains, and the yearly cycles of its trees all foster a harmonious atmosphere.

A Shinto priest rakes the gravel of a Zen garden.

WORDS TO UNDERSTAND

depose: to remove from power.

militarized: warlike or military in character and thought.

robust: strong, vigorous, and healthy.

tectonic plate: one of the massive stone sheets that forms part the Earth's crust.

wield: to possess something and have the ability to use it.

CHAPTER 1

History, Religion, and Tradition

"Dynamic" is a good word to describe Japan. As an archipelago of over 3,000 islands—some of which are volcanic—situated along the ridge of the Pacific **tectonic plate**, the nation is particularly susceptible to geological events such as earthquakes and tsunamis. The metropolitan area surrounding its capital, Tokyo, is the largest on the planet, with upwards of 36 million people. Japan has the third largest economy in the world, often leading the field when it comes to technological developments. The vibrant, fast pace of its urban life is balanced by regions of great serenity and natural beauty, such as Mount Fuji southwest of Tokyo or the Kenroku-en Garden in Kanazawa.

Japan's earliest inhabitants were Paleolithic settlers who arrived from Asia around 30,000 BCE. It is not until around 13,000 BCE, however, that we begin to get a clearer picture of the developing civilization, a culture known as the Jomon. These were hunter-gatherers who pioneered techniques of agriculture, rudimentary house construction, and clothes making. By 300 BCE, a wave of migrants known as the Yayoi began arriving in Japan. There are competing theories as to whether they originated from China or Korea. The Yayoi were responsible for introducing rice to the Japanese islands. They also improved agricultural methods and discovered new ways of working with metal. With these advances came primitive forms of government, most likely run by an emerging class of landowners.

A vase from the Jomon period.

DESIGN IN THE JOMON PERIOD

The pottery of the Jomon period is some of the oldest in the world. It is particularly noteworthy for the "cord markings" adorning the surfaces: lined designs that appear to have been applied with rope. Pots were all made by hand, without the aid of a wheel.

A more substantial historical record of Japan began developing around AD 300, as inhabitants of the Kofun period began leaving evidence of their life behind. The word *kofun* ("old mounds") refers to the large, keyhole-shaped burial mounds they constructed for their clan leaders. Items extracted from the tombs, such as weapons and armor, attest to a **militarized** society. Many different clans vied for power, but the Yamato clan proved to be the strongest. Yamato rulers established a political state with themselves as an imperial dynasty, a form of governance that continued into the Asuka period of the

The Ishibutai Kofun is the largest tomb in Japan and was built during the Asuka period.

sixth through early eighth centuries. This time in Japanese history also saw the arrival of Buddhism from China, as well as the introduction of Chinese political and cultural practices, such as bureaucratic organization (when leadership is organized into departments and levels). The Chinese writing system was also adopted during the Asuka period.

A NATIVE JAPANESE RELIGION

The native religion of Japan is known as Shintoism. It is based on Japanese myths, and its roots date as far back as the sixth century BCE. Shintoism has no sacred texts and no official founder. Practitioners are devoted to spiritual beings known as *kami*, with whom they communicate through various rituals.

The eighth century was a time of renewed stability in Japan, as a permanent capital was established in Nara, in the southern half of Honshu, the largest of Japan's main islands, in 710. Buddhism began to thrive, particularly among the upper classes, and many temples and monasteries were built. The religion had a pervasive influence on the arts and culture, setting forth new techniques in painting and sculpture. A national form of literature began to develop as writers collected ancient myths and turned them into

Daibutsu, or the Great Buddha statue, at Todai-ji Temple in Nara, Japan, is the world's largest bronze statue of the Buddha Vairocana.

poems and stories. All of this helped the Nara period come to be known as Japan's "Classical" period. Its advances continued into the Heian period, so named because the capital was relocated a bit north of Nara in Heiankyo, now Kyoto, in 794. This was truly a "golden age" of Japan, as the nation was at peace, the arts were flourishing, and new networks of roads united formerly distant locations. *The Tale of Genji*, what many consider to be the first novel, was written during this time by Murasaki Shikibu, a noblewoman who served at the imperial court. Despite such achievements, life was not always easy for village farmers, who suffered under a harsh tax system. Some landowners began employing guards known as samurai to protect their properties, creating a class of warriors that would **wield** tremendous influence over the next several centuries.

HEIAN LITERATURE

In addition to Murasaki Shikibu, another female Japanese writer made a significant contribution to world literature during the Heian Period. Sei Shonagon's *The Pillow Book* is a unique blend of diary entries, poems, and social observations written when she participated in the court of Empress Teishi.

Minomoto Yoromito was the first samurai warrior to assume power. In 1185 he relocated the capital northeast to Kamakura. He was known as a "shogun," which was the highest level of samurai. Shoguns would rule Japan for the next seven hundred years. In 1190 a new form of Buddhism called Zen arrived from China. Its teachings of rigorous mental and physical discipline greatly influenced the philosophy of the samurai class. Though they successfully defended Japan from Mongol attacks in the thirteenth century, by 1333 the Kamakura shogunate (the official name for the government of the shogun) was overthrown. A new shogunate was set up in Muromachi,

Traditional samurai armor.

Kyoto, that was much more decadent than the previous one. As Muromachi shoguns patronized the arts and developed a vibrant court culture, landowners in the outer provinces began battling for power. Known as daimyo, these lords soon tore the nation apart in a series of civil wars that would last until the mid-sixteenth century.

By 1600, a daimyo named Tokugawa Ieyasu had become the most powerful lord. He was made shogun in 1603 and moved the seat of his shogunate to Edo, which is now present-day Tokyo. He promptly created a series of laws designed to limit the power of rival daimyos. In 1639 the shogunate imposed a policy of isolation. While this effectively cut Japan off from the rest of the world, it allowed the country to strengthen its native industries and create a **robust** middle class.

The Zen Buddhist temple Kinkaku-ji (literally Temple of the Golden Pavilion) in Kyoto, Japan.

The era of stability of the Edo period lasted until 1853, when an American naval officer named Matthew Perry sailed into a port near Edo and forced the shogunate into a trade agreement. This was interpreted as a sign of weakness by the Japanese citizenry, and it unleashed a series of changes that would shake the foundations of Japan. By 1868, the shogunate was **deposed**, and power returned to the emperor. The new leadership implemented a more democratic form of government, disassembled the warrior class, and rapidly industrialized the economy.

A statue depicting Tokugawa Ieyasu, the first in the last line of shoguns, located in the Togichi Prefecture.

The horrific aftermath of the bombing of Hiroshima, Japan, in 1945. The name of the pilot who dropped the bomb and the plane he piloted are noted on the top left of the image.

Industrialization continued well into the twentieth century, when Japan became recognized as a world power. It participated victoriously in World War I on the side of the Allies. With Japan's alliance with the Axis Powers in World War II and the bombing of U.S. forces at Pearl Harbor in Hawaii in 1941, the United States declared war on Japan and entered the war on the side of the Allied Powers. The dropping of atomic bombs on Hiroshima and Nagasaki at the end of the war in 1945 left Japan in ruins. The nation demonstrated resilience, however, quickly drafting a new democratic constitution, with the cooperation and oversight of the United States and other Allied powers, that widened the scope of rights for citizens. Workers sprung back to make Japan the second largest economy in the world throughout the second half of the century.

TEXT-DEPENDENT QUESTIONS

1. How has the religion of Buddhism influenced Japanese culture over the years?

2. In what ways has the Japanese political system, especially its forms of leadership, changed throughout history?

3. What caused Japan's movement toward modernization in the nineteenth century? How did this movement take form?

RESEARCH PROJECTS

1. Select either an emperor or a shogun from the history of Japan. Research his life and times, and write a brief biography that includes his leadership style, the advances (or setbacks) he brought to Japan, and the characteristics of his rule.

2. Research the relationship between America and Japan since the end of World War II, focusing particularly on the cultural exchanges between the two nations in the era of globalization. Write a brief report summarizing your findings.

A traditional Japanese garden.

A family going to a wedding at the Meiji Jingu Shrine in Tokyo.

WORDS TO UNDERSTAND

aesthetically: relating to aesthetics, or the study of beauty and its forms; in a beautiful way.

decorum: politeness and proper conduct in a given situation.

manipulate: to handle or control something with skill.

nuanced: having small and subtle variations of meaning.

ritualize: to mark or perform with specific behaviors or observances.

CHAPTER **2**

Family and Friends

Japanese social customs are very **nuanced**. Even something as simple as nonverbal body language is subject to various unwritten rules; for instance, it is considered respectful to maintain upright posture when speaking with someone. Such customs carry over when spending time with families and friends. The Japanese people place a high value on the harmony of their social life and avoid openly criticizing one another or engaging in behavior that would cause discomfort. One's individual behavior is seen as contributing to a greater good; therefore, it is important to treat everyone with kindness and **decorum**.

A traditional tea ceremony, or *chanoyu*, takes place here in a garden.

One way of spending time with family and friends is the traditional Japanese tea ceremony, called a *chanoyu*. Tea itself was not native to Japan but brought from China around the ninth century. Over time, Japanese monks who had traveled in China introduced various methods of brewing and serving tea. By the sixteenth century, these practices had evolved into a ritual favored by the ruling elite as a way of bonding with one another. Their gatherings took on spiritual overtones: guests were expected to leave their worldly concerns behind and be fully in the moment, and hosts would supply **aesthetically** pleasing objects that demonstrated proper proportion and balance.

SHARING MEALS

As in many cultures, the Japanese enjoy sharing meals with family and friends. There are many rules of etiquette to ensure people feel comfortable and to foster a feeling of gratitude. For instance, it is considered impolite to begin eating before saying *itadakimasu*, which translates to "I humbly receive." At the conclusion of a meal, diners say *gochisosama*: "Thank you for the meal."

The tea ceremony today stays true to these principles. It begins with guests washing their hands and mouths as a means of purification. They remove their shoes, then enter the room where the ceremony will be held. The door to the room is a little over three feet high, forcing the guests to crouch. Once inside, the host lights a small charcoal fire to eventually boil water. A meal or sweet snack is served. After the meal the guests are dismissed so the host can tidy the room. When the guests return, the host puts a kettle of water on the fire and cleans the bowls and whatever implements will be used to make the tea. He or she stirs powdered tea into the kettle with a special bamboo whisk called a *chasen*. Everyone drinks the tea from a single cup, which is passed around with very precise motions and bows.

AN IMPORTANT GESTURE

Bowing is the customary form of greeting friends and family in Japan. The deeper the bow, the more formal the greeting. There are numerous rules governing how one should bow, depending on the occasion, the social status of the people involved, and whether or not the bow may be one of apology. It is such an important tradition in Japan that children are taught how to properly execute a bow from an early age.

Two women share their lunch at a restaurant in Hakone, Kanakawa, Japan.

A traditional Shinto wedding ceremony at the Meiji-Jinju Shrine, pictured here. A Shinto priest conducts the ceremony, attended only by close family members.

The tea ceremony's atmosphere of peaceful, harmonious communication is replicated in other Japanese social customs such as gift giving. Exchanging gifts with family, friends, and even strangers is a part of daily life, and people put great thought into what they give and how they choose to present it. Gifts are given at every conceivable occasion. Besides birthdays, weddings, and graduations, there is a practice called *okaeshi* in which someone who has received a gift gives something in return. Ochugen occurs in early July; this is a special time to send gifts to one's parents and employers as a sign of gratitude. A related holiday, Oseibo, takes place in December. Here, people give gifts to those who have helped them in some way throughout the year. *Omiyage* is the tradition of bringing back souvenirs, usually edible goods, from one's travels to share with family and friends.

CHANGING TRADITIONS

As Japan has adopted some Western cultural practices, so have wedding traditions changed. Whereas weddings were traditionally held in Shinto temples and were very ornate affairs, today many couples opt to marry in smaller venues designed to look like Christian chapels. Other Western practices such as the exchange of rings and the post-wedding honeymoon are popular as well.

In Japanese culture, the way a gift is wrapped is as important as the gift itself, and it is considered impolite to give an unwrapped gift. The custom of *furoshiki* has been in practice for over a thousand years. It involves wrapping a gift in a single piece of fabric tied

Traditionally wrapped gifts.

in an artful way. *Origata* is a similar practice, except that it utilizes different types of paper instead of fabric. The paper must not be cut during the course of wrapping but **manipulated** in such a way that the object is concealed. Different colored papers represent different things and should appropriately match the tone of the occasion. For instance, yellow symbolizes courage and good cheer; green, fertility and renewal; and black, mournfulness or mystery.

FAMILY RESPONSIBILITIES

Traditionally, Japanese children care for their parents as they get older. The responsibility to take in an aging parent tends to fall to the oldest son, with his wife as the primary caretaker. In recent years, this practice has grown more difficult as the demands of the global economy force daughters-in-law to work rather than stay at home.

A grandfather, father, and young son reading together. Care for aging parents is still an important value in Japanese society.

A popular place for family and friends to meet is the *sento*, or local bathhouse. The tradition of the *sento* dates back to when few Japanese homes were equipped with private baths. Though this has changed over the years, the *sento* still remains a part of Japanese culture. Like the tea ceremony, time spent at the bathhouse is highly **ritualized** and helps bring people together.

Upon entering the *sento*, guests are separated by gender. They must wash before plunging into the baths, which are designed for soaking, not cleaning the body. No chemical products such as soaps or shampoos are allowed to touch the water. Multiple types of baths are set to various temperatures. There are often windows placed high on the walls above the baths so as to let in natural light, as well as murals adorning the walls depicting pastoral scenes. As they relax in the water, family and friends take advantage of the informal atmosphere to catch up with one another. **Socioeconomic** barriers are broken down in the *sento*, as the shared immersion unites people of all walks of life. Some modern *sento* have come to resemble fitness clubs or day spas, with exercise equipment, saunas and steam rooms, and other amenities.

A woman tests the water in a traditional *sento* bath.

TEXT-DEPENDENT QUESTIONS

1. In what ways does the Japanese tea ceremony create an atmosphere of calmness and order?

2. How does the tradition of gift giving demonstrate the importance of human relationships in Japanese culture?

3. What are some ritualistic elements of the *sento*?

RESEARCH PROJECTS

1. Research an event that marks a person's life in some way— a baptism, birthday, or wedding are some examples—and how it is celebrated in Japan. Write a brief report summarizing your findings, including how traditions differ from those in the United States.

2. Research other Japanese dining customs, such as the polite way to use chopsticks or how to properly signal that you are finished with your meal. Make a table with three columns: one for describing the custom, one describing the occasion it is used in, and the third, noting similar or contrasting customs in the United States.

A Japanese father takes his children for a bicycle ride.

Sushi with a seaweed salad.

WORDS TO UNDERSTAND

fermentation: a process in which microorganisms such as yeast or bacteria break a substance down, usually producing heat or gas.

innumerable: unable to be counted.

preoccupation: something of great concern.

probiotic: a microorganism that has health benefits when consumed.

unpretentious: modest or humble.

CHAPTER **3**

Food and Drink

The cuisine of Japan is characterized by its fresh, seasonally appropriate ingredients and artful presentation. A typical Japanese meal is a feast for the eyes as much as for the stomach, with colors and textures arranged in careful harmony. Rice is a staple and the basis of most dishes, and fish, seaweed, and other "fruits of the ocean" are prepared in creative ways. Pickling is a popular way of preserving vegetables so they can be served year-round. In all, food is a Japanese **preoccupation**: many citizens will travel for miles just to try a dish specific to a certain region of their country.

Undoubtedly, the best-known item of Japanese cuisine throughout the world is sushi. Sushi's origins go back thousands of years to Southeast Asia,

Sushi comes in many sizes, shapes, and even colors.

where cooks noticed that wrapping salted fish in cooked rice triggered a **fermentation** process that preserved the fish. The technique spread to Japan by the eighth century. Over time, the Japanese began to eat the rice along with the fish instead of discarding it, as was the common practice. By the fifteenth century, they realized the fish did not have to be fully fermented before consuming. This allowed them to experiment with a new technique of speeding up fermentation: flavoring the rice with vinegar, adding the fish, and eating it a few hours later. When a chef named Hanaya Yohei discarded the fermentation process altogether in the nineteenth century, serving freshly caught fish raw with a bit of vinegar-flavored rice, modern sushi was born.

A CHINESE IMPORT

Noodles are also important in Japanese cuisine, with many variations, such as soba and udon. Ramen, another type, was imported from China during the latter part of the nineteenth century and has spread in popularity across the globe, including packets of the instant ramen so popular for quick meals in the United States.

Ramen soup can include vegetables, pieces of pork, and even a hard-boiled egg.

Today sushi is prepared in a method similar to Yohei's, though there have been some variations along the way. A very popular type of sushi is *maki*, or rolled sushi. Here, the chef lays out a sheet of dried seaweed on a small bamboo mat. He or she then puts down a layer of vinegared rice; the rice is purposefully very sticky so it is easy to spread and roll. Another technique is to wet one's hands with vinegar and water before handling the rice. Atop the rice goes the filling of fish or vegetables. The mat is rolled so all the ingredients are compressed and the seaweed seals around them. When the chef unrolls the mat, he or she cuts the sushi into bite-sized pieces. They are traditionally served with soy sauce for dipping, a strong-flavored condiment called wasabi, and pickled ginger to help cleanse the palate.

Besides *maki*, there are many other types of sushi. *Nigiri* is a small bite of rice with a piece of raw fish on top. *Temaki* are sheets of seaweed rolled into conical shapes and stuffed with fish,

Example of *temaki* sushi.

Rolling up sushi *maki* with a bamboo mat.

Miso paste, tofu, and soy sauce all come from soybeans.

rice, and vegetables. *Oshizushi*, or "pressed sushi," is made by compressing fish and rice together in a rectangular box for a precise presentation.

A very versatile ingredient at the center of Japanese cuisine is the **unpretentious** soybean. This legume is used not only in main dishes, but also to make such condiments as soy sauce and miso. Soy sauce, called shoyu, is made of soybeans, wheat, salt, water, and mold cultures that aid in the fermentation process. At the end of a six-month fermentation cycle, the liquid is strained off of the solid ingredients, pasteurized, and bottled. Miso is made by fermenting soybeans, salt, and grains such as rice or barley. When everything is blended, it produces a paste that can be used as a flavoring agent. A soup made with miso, fish stock, vegetables, and tofu—a product made from the curds of soy milk—is a common appetizer in Japanese homes.

THE HUMBLE SOYBEAN

An even simpler soybean appetizer is *edamame*: the beans are boiled right in their pods, cooled, and salted. *Natto* is more of an acquired taste: plain fermented soybeans, often eaten for breakfast, that have a stringy, sticky texture and a pungent odor. *Natto* can be eaten alone, with rice, or—in a more modern way—with toast. It may also be used in sushi or served atop noodles.

Salted *edamame*—soybeans in the pod—make a healthy snack or appetizer.

Tofu itself has **innumerable** uses. Little is known of its history, other than that it originated in ancient China and was brought to Japan by Buddhist priests who studied there in the eighth century. It was instantly popular, as Japan had a high proportion of vegetarians, and tofu is an excellent source of meatless protein. By 1782 there was even a cookbook, *Tofu Hyakuchin*, that listed one hundred recipes centered around the food! Tofu comes in a variety of textures and densities, from soft and silken to solid and firm. Different varieties are better for different preparatory methods. For instance, silken tofu is often used instead of dairy products in desserts, while firm tofu is better for grilling or frying. The flavor of tofu itself is very mild, and thus it can blend well with many different ingredients.

Popular miso soup recipes contain wakame (an edible seaweed), tofu, made from soy milk, and scallions.

Japanese tempura with soy sauce and sake.

A GIFT FROM PORTUGAL

Tempura is a dish that was imported to Japan by Portuguese missionaries in the sixteenth century. It is now so thoroughly associated with Japanese cuisine that many people are unaware of its origins. Tempura consists of vegetables or fish dipped in a light wheat-based batter and deep fried. Squash, shrimp, and sweet potatoes are popular foods used to make tempura.

When it comes to washing down all these delectable dishes, the Japanese have a variety of beverages to choose from. As evidenced by the importance placed on the tea ceremony, hot tea is a very common choice. Not all "tea" is made with tea leaves, however: *mugicha* is brewed with roasted barley and is usually sipped cold as a summer refresher, *soba cha* is made with roasted buckwheat, and *sakura* uses pickled cherry blossoms. *Kombucha* (not to be confused with the fermented beverage of the same English name) is powdered kelp (a type of brown seaweed called kombu in Japanese) stirred into hot water.

DRINKING VINEGAR

The Japanese have valued the health properties of vinegar for hundreds of years. By adding natural flavors such as fruit, honey, or mint, the Japanese over time have created vinegar drinks that harness its natural benefits while making it more palatable.

Two modern health drinks are very popular in Japan, where physical fitness is highly valued. Yakult is a **probiotic** drink made by adding a healthy strain of bacteria to skim milk and then fermenting the mixture. Sugar is added to balance flavor, and other natural flavors such as apple or grape may be added. Invented in 1935, Yakult is believed to aid the immune and digestive systems. *Aojiru*, meaning "green drink," is a kale-based vegetable drink that contains many important nutrients. A doctor first developed it in 1943 as a means of improving his family's health during wartime. Though the taste is rather bitter, it remains a popular nutritional supplement for thousands of Japanese.

TEXT-DEPENDENT QUESTIONS

1. What are some products in Japanese cuisine that employ the fermentation process?

2. What are some popular soy-based products in Japanese cuisine?

RESEARCH PROJECTS

1. Select a region of Japan (e.g., Kansai, Tokohu, or Chubu), and research its cuisine. Write a brief report summarizing your findings, including famous dishes of that region and ingredients native to the area.

2. Look in the international section of a grocery store or look at a Japanese online grocery store (such as http://www.marukaiestore.com/) and put together a shopping list for a Japanese meal, along with a final menu.

Yasai roll.

The Tokyo Motor Show in Adaiba.

WORDS TO UNDERSTAND

maritime: relating to the sea; in close proximity to the sea.

parity: the state of being equal.

radioactive: relating to radioactivity, a powerful form of energy that occurs when an element spontaneously emits particles.

tempestuous: characterized by stormy, conflicting emotions.

tsunami: a giant wave caused by movements of the earth, such as an earthquake or volcanic eruption.

CHAPTER 4

School, Work, and Industry

Few nations place as much of an emphasis on education and industriousness as Japan. Being a nation that values individual contributions toward a greater good, Japan ensures that its students are ready to contribute to the workforce. Japan has a long tradition of economic resiliency, such as when it grew to become the second largest economy in the world after the traumatic experience of World War II. Its manufacturing, technology, and transportation sectors are the envy of many industrialized nations. At the same time, the Japanese value their long history of traditional handicrafts, including pottery, lacquerware, and hand-painted fans.

Japanese students in their school uniforms.

Japanese education is of a very high standard. It is broken down into six years of elementary school, three years of junior high school, and three years of senior high school. Elementary and junior high school are compulsory, and close to 100 percent of students go on to senior high school. Technical schools are also available at the senior level for those wishing to pursue specific careers such as engineering. After high school, nearly half of Japanese students elect to continue their studies at a four-year university. Because the Japanese government monitors each element of the educational system very closely, there is a **parity** of student success between various regions of the country. This is borne out by Japan's 99 percent literacy rate and 95 percent high school graduation rate.

UNIFORM DRESSING

School uniforms are required in many Japanese junior and senior high schools. The traditional Japanese school uniform is based on Western-style military clothing: a blouse with a sailor-style collar and a skirt for girls, and a pants and jacket combination with a "stand-up" collar for boys. Students are also required to wear *uwabaki*, or special slippers, while inside the school.

A day in a Japanese elementary school is slightly different from that of its American counterpart. Students share a single room, and all subjects are generally taught by the same teacher. In addition to standard subjects such as language, math, and science, students are also exposed to the Japanese arts of calligraphy (carefully painting characters of the Japanese language) and haiku (a form of poetry with a precise amount of syllables in each line). Rather than emphasize the individual, Japanese teachers strive to show the benefits of sharing duties as a group. For instance, students are often responsible for cleaning their own classrooms at the end of the day, and during lunch rotating groups of students serve one another.

One area where Japan's industriousness has made it a world leader is that of rail travel. Japan is home to the Shinkansen bullet train, one of the fastest trains in the world. It is capable of going 200 miles per hour. The high-speed Shinkansen railway network connects Japan's major cities along nearly fifteen thousand miles of track. What is truly amazing is that the system has been in place since 1964, when its rapid speeds enabled greater communication between various parts of the country. It is known for its extreme punctuality, with arrivals and departures often accurate to the second. Its roomy, clean

Students talk on the train going home from school.

Akihabara in Tokyo, a famous shopping district for electronics, computers, video games, and other modern gadgetry.

interiors are another popular feature. Today 143 million passengers ride the Shinkansen every year. In 2013 tests began on the latest version of the bullet train, the L0 Series, a "maglev" train, short for "magnetic levitation," which uses the power of magnetism to raise the train and push it forward on the guiderails. The L0 Series is anticipated to reach speeds of 310 miles per hour!

Though many of its citizens utilize rail travel, Japan is still among the top three automobile-producing countries in the world: 9.9 million cars are manufactured there each year. Models such as Toyota, Honda, and Suzuki all originated in Japan. In addition to autos, Honda is among the world's leaders in motorcycle sales and manufacturing.

Just as it is a leader in auto manufacturing, Japan excels in computer-related technology. And despite losing ground to other countries, including South Korea and Taiwan, Japan is renowned for its electronic industry. Many innovations in our digital world have originated in Japanese companies, including the Sony Walkman and first LCD screens (developed by Sharp).

ELECTRONICS WORLD

The electronics district in Tokyo, Akihabara, is evidence of Japan's obsession with electronic and digital life. It is a world-renown shopping district where consumers can buy anything from computers and electronic gadgets to anime videos and *manga* comics.

With Japan being an island nation, **maritime** activities such as ferry services and fisheries are naturally quite important. Japan's main ferry routes provide an alternative form of transport between the four main islands (Honshu, Hokkaido, Kyushu, and Shikoku), as well as a means of getting to some of the smaller islands that would be otherwise inaccessible. There are also international routes connecting Japan to Russia, China, and South Korea.

The Japanese fishing industry is in the midst of transition. Years of overfishing have depleted the oceans and endangered many species. The 2011 Tohoku earthquake triggered a **tsunami** that devastated northern Japan: thousands of people died or were injured, and the flooding caused a meltdown at the Fukushima Daiichi Nuclear Power Plant. The runoff of **radioactive** material made its way into the ocean, resulting in extensive pollution. Fishermen could not continue working in the area, and both domestic and international consumers began to distrust the safety of fish caught off the coast of Japan. Though there are some ideological clashes between environmentalists who wish to see Japan incorporate more sustainable fishing practices and fishermen dependent on time-tested methods, both parties recognize that changes must be made to preserve the industry for the long term.

The *Nisshin Maru* is the largest ship in the Japanese whaling fleet and the world's only whale factory ship. It is pictured here in 2008 at the docks in Kagoshima City during a whaling festival.

A less **tempestuous** sector of the Japanese economy is that of traditional handicrafts. Among the most revered worldwide is Japanese lacquerware. Lacquer is a substance made from the sap of the Japanese lacquer tree. As the tree is related to the poison ivy family, lacquer is highly toxic. When refined, it can be applied to the surface of an object to give it a hard, shiny finish, much like a plastic coating. Several coats must be used for it to be effective, making the process very time consuming.

TEMARI TOYS

Temari are another popular handicraft in Japan. These small toy balls, made of scraps of old fabric (usually that of discarded robes called kimonos), were introduced to Japan from China in the seventh century. Soon they progressed into a Japanese art form, as embroiderers stitched them with intricate, colorful patterns. *Temari* are still in production today, and are often given as "good luck" charms.

The most common objects to lacquer are wood, leather, and paper. As the artist applies the lacquer, he or she decorates the object between coats with gold or silver powder or mother-of-pearl inlay. Sometimes natural materials such as seashells are used. The finished products are not only beautiful to behold but also functional: bowls, plates, tools for tea ceremonies, and furniture are only some of the objects used for lacquerware. Bento boxes—small, compartmentalized boxes used to hold the various items of a Japanese meal—are often decorated with lacquer and hand-painted designs.

A traditional lacquered box.

Temari made from kimono fabric and embroidery.

TEXT-DEPENDENT QUESTIONS

1. What are some ways in which Japanese education differs from American education?

2. What are some notable advances of the Japanese rail system?

3. How does the proximity to the sea influence the Japanese economy, and what challenges does it present?

RESEARCH PROJECTS

1. Research an element of the electronics industry in Japan, such as its contributions to computer, video game, or digital camera production. Write a brief report outlining the history of this branch of the industry, how it has evolved, and what innovations it is currently making.

2. Research another small-scale industry or handicraft native to Japan. Write a brief report summarizing its history, how it is practiced, and the challenges it might face due to large-scale competitors in the age of globalization.

A train leaving the Shinkansen station.

Taiko drummers.

WORDS TO UNDERSTAND

hearken: to recall an earlier subject or instance of something.

juxtaposition: to place two or more things beside each other.

meditative: relating to meditation, the process of focusing or clarifying one's thoughts.

mindfulness: the quality or state of being mindful, that is, of giving careful and considerate attention to something.

pare: to cut away excess.

CHAPTER **5**

Arts and Entertainment

Japan is home to many diverse artistic traditions. From the folding paper art known as origami to the ink wash painting known as *sumi-e*, Japanese art emphasizes **mindfulness**, patience, and fluidity of technique. Final works are marked by a cohesive elegance that aims to mimic the balance found in nature. These principles are important in Japanese literature as well, particularly in its poetry.

The crane, a classic example of Japanese origami.

Forms such as haiku attempt to present the natural world with great simplicity and clarity of vision. While Japanese art is known for its serenity, contemporary mainstream entertainment is less so: amusement parks, video games, and the sing-along craze of karaoke are all popular diversions in modern Japan.

Two sumo wrestlers practice during the Grand Sumo Tournament in 2009.

For hundreds of years, the sport of sumo wrestling has been a source of fun and excitement for the Japanese. One of Japan's most ancient martial arts, sumo began as a Shinto ritual in which performers entertained spirits called *kami*. By the eighth century, the sport had become popular among the ruling elite, and matches were held for the imperial court. However, it was not until the Edo period of the seventeenth century that sumo found mass appeal. The ring, or *dohyo*, was incorporated around this time, and tournaments were held that attracted large audiences. Wood-block prints depicting famous sumo wrestlers were sought-after collectibles, much like baseball cards are today.

The rules of sumo are famously simple: the loser of the bout is the first wrestler to be forced outside the ring or to touch the ground with any part of his body other than the soles of his feet. The ring is approximately fifteen feet in diameter, and the ground is made of clay and topped with a dusting of sand. At the start of each match the wrestlers purify the ring with salt, a tradition that **hearkens** back to the sport's Shinto roots. The famously full-bodied wrestlers crouch, facing each other, and breathe in unison. The moment both place their fists upon the ground, the match begins. A match usually lasts no longer than a few seconds, though they can go several minutes or longer. While the movements of the wrestlers may appear haphazard, they actually take a great deal of concentration to execute properly.

THE SUMO LIFESTYLE

Sumo wrestlers live together in "stables" headed by "stable masters" who govern all aspects of their training regimen, including their diet and sleep schedules. There is a division in the stable between the younger amateur wrestlers and senior professional ones, with the junior wrestlers assigned menial maintenance tasks. It is nearly impossible for an outsider to be granted access to a stable; if a tourist is allowed in, he or she must be accompanied by a native Japanese speaker.

Concentration and focus are apparent in a quite different Japanese practice: the art of ink wash painting, also known as *sumi-e* or *suiboku-ga*. The style originated in China during the Tang dynasty of the seventh through early tenth centuries. In the fourteenth century, it was brought to Japan by Zen Buddhist priests who valued its commitment to depicting only the essential elements of a picture. Such an aim meshed well with Zen Buddhist goals of **paring** life down to its essential components, being disciplined, and developing a high degree of focus. Thus many Zen monks, such as Shubun and his student Sesshu, were the leading practitioners of the art form throughout the fifteenth and sixteenth centuries.

Ink wash painting *Shukei-sansui,* or *Autumn Landscape,* by Sesshu Toyo (1420–1506).

Two friends sing at a fun evening of karaoke.

SING ALONG!

Karaoke is a form of Japanese entertainment that has gained popularity worldwide. The word *karaoke* comes from a combination of *kara*, "empty," and *okesutora*, "orchestra." Participants sing along to prerecorded instrumental versions of their favorite songs, with the lyrics projected on screens in front of them. "Karaoke boxes" are small rooms containing karaoke equipment. Groups of friends can rent them by the hour and relax by trading songs.

Traditional *sumi-e* uses four tools: an ink stone, an ink stick, a brush, and paper. The painter makes his or her own ink in a **meditative** fashion, carefully adding drops of water to a depression in the ink stone. He or she then swirls the ink stick—made of soot from a burnt pine tree combined with resin and compressed—in the water in a circular motion to create the ink. Brushes are usually made of bamboo with some type of animal hair for bristles. Often paper made from rice or bamboo fibers is used, as they are neither too rugged nor too flimsy. There are four basic brushstrokes utilized in *sumi-e*. The painter's aim is to convey the spirit of the subject rather than its physical appearance. He or she will deliberate at length before making a single brushstroke. Landscapes with mountains, rivers, and other natural features are traditional subjects and may include a human presence in the form of a lone pilgrim.

PERFORMING WITH MASKS

Noh theater is a traditional dramatic art of Japan. The plots and pacing of Noh plays are often very slow and methodical. They may be based on historical, literary, or mythological events. The main character, or *shite*, utilizes a mask to clue the audience in as to what type of person he is. This requires great subtlety on the part of the actor, who must be precise in his movements to indicate different emotions.

A close cousin of *sumi-e* is the literary form of haiku. A haiku was originally the first stanza of a longer type of poem called a *renga*, but by the seventeenth century poets began composing them alone. A haiku follows very specific rules. It has three lines; the first and third line are five syllables, and the mid-

A Japanese stage group performs a Noh drama in Solo, Java, Indonesia. Noh originated in the fourteenth-century Muromachi period.

dle line is seven syllables. Within this constricted space, it aims to present an image or emotion with great precision. It may use a **juxtaposition** of images to create a certain mood. Haiku favors images of the natural world and often illustrates a moment when the poet feels unified with nature.

A HUMOROUS POET

Among Matsuo Basho's most revered poems is "Furuike ya/kawazu tobikomu/mizu no oto." While it is difficult to render the exact syllable counts in English, this was translated by Donald Keene as "The ancient pond/a frog leaps in/the sound of water." Basho was not without a sense of humor: another famous haiku is "Iza saraba/yukimi ni korobu/tokoromade," or "Now then, let's go out/to enjoy the snow . . . until/I slip and fall."

A statue of haiku master Matsuo Basho at the Chuson-ji Temple, Hiraizumi, Iwate Prefecture, Japan.

Of the Japanese haiku poets, Matsuo Basho is the best known. He was born in 1644 in Ueno and studied poetry at a young age. In his twenties he supported himself with work as a teacher and began composing his own poems. Soon these poems found their way to leading literary and intellectual figures of the time. In order to focus more intensely on his work, he moved into a small home by himself and began practicing Zen meditation. Sadly, the house burned down in 1682, leaving Basho devastated. Two years later he began traveling around Japan, recording his impressions in books that combined poetry and prose. Works such as *Spring Days* remain classics of world literature for their clear language and depth of feeling. Shortly after setting off for the last of his travels, Basho died in the fall of 1694.

TEXT-DEPENDENT QUESTIONS

1. In what ways do the Japanese arts—visual, verbal, and martial—value precision in expression?

2. How did Zen Buddhism influence *sumi-e* painting?

3. What are some common subjects of both *sumi-e* painting and haiku?

RESEARCH PROJECTS

1. Research a form of modern-day mass entertainment in Japan, such as karaoke, amusement parks, or movies. Write a brief report discussing the history of this type of entertainment, why it is valued by the Japanese, and how it is changing in the twenty-first century.

2. Research more about Noh drama as well as another form of Japanese theater, such as Kabuki or Bunraku. Prepare a table comparing characteristics of both, including such aspects as the history, origins, major works, its current popularity today, and what special costumes or props, if any, are used.

Lanterns on display in a shop.

Shirakawago Village, Japan.

WORDS TO UNDERSTAND

conducive: making a situation easier or more likely to happen.

mechanization: the transition from handwork to machine-driven production.

minimalist: the quality of using few elements to achieve a desired effect.

pagoda: a type of tower native to East Asia with curving, protruding roofs that divide each floor.

CHAPTER **6**

Cities, Towns, and the Countryside

Between its thriving urban centers, fertile agricultural regions, and remote coastlines of staggering natural beauty, Japan's landscape is one of great physical contrasts. Its cities are home to some of the most groundbreaking architecture in the world, while in the countryside residents continue to use ancient methods such as terrace farming to grow rice and other crops. The tradition of the Japanese garden ties the rural and urban spheres together, as gardens are designed to provide a "refuge" from the hustle and bustle of human interaction. While most westerners know the Japanese archipelago for its four largest islands, over four hundred of its thousands of smaller islands are also inhabited, with fishing and tourism being their primary economies.

The Tokyo Skytree along the Sumida River (left) and a closeup of its spire (right).

Dominating the Tokyo skyline is a television and radio broadcasting tower known as the Tokyo Skytree. At 2,722 feet (830 m), the Skytree is the tallest tower in the world and the second tallest structure overall, after the Burj Khalifa skyscraper in Dubai. Its two observation decks allow for sweeping views of the cityscape. There are also restaurants, shopping areas, and even an aquarium located at the base. Construction began in 2008 and was completed four years later. Due to the Japanese archipelago's **susceptibility** to natural disasters, special care was taken to make sure the Skytree could withstand an earthquake. A reinforced concrete pillar runs up the center of the tower and is attached to the exterior frame with special shock absorbers known as dampers. These "cushion" the building against excessive shaking.

A TREE IN THE SKY

Even the colors of the lights used to illuminate the Tokyo Skytree on its inaugural night were rooted in traditional Japanese symbolism. Architects chose to use a special blue (*iki*) that represents purity, suffused with lavender (*miyabi*) to signify elegance. The two colors helped preserve the cultural memory of Japan's deep past even while unveiling its most modern structure.

What is unique about the Skytree is that its modern design incorporates elements of traditional Japanese architecture. For instance, the classic Japanese **pagoda** also has a central pillar called a *shinbashira*. The shape of the Skytree's metal beams was inspired by Buddhist temples from the Nara and Heian periods, and the arcs of the braces between the beams mirror the arcs of Japanese swords. The color of the tower is derived from a traditional Japanese hue known as *aijiro*. This pale shade of indigo blue gives the tower a special glow when set against the bright Japanese sky.

A "garden" in the Japanese sense is not necessarily a place to grow food, but rather a portion of the landscape modified to be aesthetically pleasing and **conducive** to contemplation. There are several types of Japanese gardens, including *karesansui*, or rock gardens; *tsukiyama*, or "hill gardens" that incorporate more varied terrain; and *chaniwa*, which are affiliated with the houses used for tea ceremonies.

The tradition of Japanese gardens dates back to ancient Shinto culture, when people would designate sacred spaces by spreading pebbles in an artful fashion. The influence of Chinese Buddhism in the sixth century brought new techniques, such as the addition of small ponds or the redirection of streams to

Gardens at the Adachi Museum of Art in Japan.

make waterfalls. By the eighth century, builders were adding bridges and pavilions to these bodies of water, and gardens were used as much for entertainment as contemplation. This changed with the advent of samurai influence, when gardens became more **minimalist** in their design. By the seventeenth century, however, the rulers of the Edo period had reverted back to the preferences of their ancestors and began constructing large "strolling gardens." These were almost like parks in their use of winding paths and varied scenery.

RICE FARMING IN TRANSITION

Terrace farming is the ancient practice of shaping land into a series of "steps" to grow food. The method has many benefits, both environmental (such as the ability to naturally conserve rainwater) and in terms of efficiency. Japanese rice growers have utilized terrace farming for generations, though many farms have switched to large, flat paddies that involve the use of pesticides. Some farmers see this **mechanization** as a danger to public health and have worked to preserve rice terraces.

View from the Hanami-bashi Bridge at the Kenroku-en Garden in Kanazawa.

Noted for its abundance of alpine flowers, Rebun is only 31 square miles (80 square km) and home to 4,300 people. The northernmost inhabited island in Japan, it is seen here from Mount Rishiri on Rishiri Island.

While originally designed for the recreation of the aristocratic class, gardens are now a part of Japanese culture available to all. Nowhere is this more apparent than with the "Three Great Gardens": Kenroku-en in Kanazawa, Kairaku-en in Mito, and Koraku-en in Okayama. Said to be the most famous gardens in Japan, visitors flock to experience their beauty during all seasons of the year. Each demonstrates traditionally valued qualities: Kenroku-en balances solitary and communal space, Kairaku-en features plum trees and flowers of various colors, and Koraku-en creates a welcoming environment with varied attractions for guests.

Set apart from the more populated areas of Japan are the northernmost inhabited islands of the archipelago, Rishiri and Rebun. Known as the "Floating Islands of Flowers," both are known for their breathtaking natural scenery and unspoiled nature. Much of this has been preserved by the 82-square-mile (212-square-km) Rishiri-Rebun-Sarobetsu National Park, which incorporates both islands as well as a stretch of coastline along Hokkaido Island. The park is a fertile fishing area and draws many hikers, who access the islands via a three-hour ferry ride from the port of Wakkani.

Rishiri is the larger of the two islands. It is nearly perfectly circular. Its main geographic feature is Mount Rishiri, a dormant volcano that rises 5,600 feet (1,707 m). The mountain's shape recalls that of the more famous (and Japan's tallest) Mount Fuji, on Honshu not far southwest of Tokyo, so the two are often linked in the Japanese imagination. The island is also home to many species of alpine plants. Just over five thousand residents call Rishiri home, and they are divided almost equally between two towns, Rishiri and *Rishirfuji*.

AN ISLAND FROM THE PAST

Another unique Japanese island is Aogashima, located 222 miles (357 km) south of Tokyo in the Phillippine Sea. Created by ancient volcanic activity, the small island (3.4 square miles [8.8 square km]) is home to 200 residents and is governed by the city of Tokyo. It is only accessible by helicopter or boat. Such remoteness, however, has allowed the tropical island to be well preserved throughout the centuries.

Rebun is significantly smaller, at 31 square miles (80 square km), though its alpine vegetation rivals that of Rishiri for diversity and natural beauty. Approximately 4,300 people live on Rebun; like Rishiri, their primary means of employment are either helping with the tourism industry or fishing. A special "eight-hour" hiking trail **wends** its way across the island, allowing for views of Rishiri and the surrounding seas.

View of Yokohama city and Mt. Fuji.

TEXT-DEPENDENT QUESTIONS

1. In what ways does the Tokyo Skytree utilize traditional Japanese building methods?

2. What are some reasons for the importance of gardens throughout Japanese history?

3. Why are remote regions of the Japanese archipelago, such as Rebun and Rishiri, such noteworthy destinations?

RESEARCH PROJECTS

1. Research one of the forty-seven prefectures (i.e., administrative divisions) of Japan. Write a brief report summarizing your findings, including a history of the prefecture, facts about its current population, its geographic features, and how it contributes to the Japanese nation.

2. Research one of the many famous mountains in Japan. Write a brief report summarizing its geological history, its relationship to the surrounding landscape (including whether it is part of a larger chain), and its cultural significance.

The Hikone Castle in Shiga.

FURTHER RESEARCH

Online

View statistics, maps, and a brief history about Japan on the Central Intelligence Agency's World Factbook website (https://www.cia.gov/library/publications/the-world-factbook/geos/ja.html).

The Japan National Tourism Organization website (http://www.jnto.go.jp) offers information for people interested in visiting or learning about Japan.

"Experience Japanese Culture" (http://www.jnto.go.jp/eng/indepth/cultural/experience/) is also hosted by the Japan National Tourism Organization and discusses many forms of Japanese culture.

Japan-Guide (http://www.japan-guide.com/) is a comprehensive travel site, covering all sorts of topics relating to Japan, including latest news, photos of popular destinations, and detailed maps.

Samurai Archives (http://www.samurai-archives.com/) features all sorts of information about the history and practices of samurai culture.

Books

Basho, Matsuo. *The Complete Haiku*. Tokyo: Kodansha USA, 2013.

Dougill, John. *Japan's World Heritage Sites: Unique Culture, Unique Nature*. North Clarendon, VT: Tuttle, 2014.

Henshall, Kenneth. *A History of Japan: From Stone Age to Superpower*. 3rd ed. New York: Palgrave Macmillan, 2012.

Kajiyama, Sumiko. *Cool Japan: A Guide to Tokyo, Kyoto, Tohoku and Japanese Culture Past and Present*. New York: Museyon, 2013.

Sosnoski, Daniel. *Introduction to Japanese Culture*. North Clarendon, VT: Tuttle, 2014.

NOTE TO EDUCATORS: This book contains both imperial and metric measurements as well as references to global practices and trends in an effort to encourage the student to gain a worldly perspective. We, as publishers, feel it's our role to give young adults the tools they need to thrive in a global society.

SERIES GLOSSARY

ancestral: relating to ancestors, or relatives who have lived in the past.

archaeologist: a scientist that investigates past societies by digging in the earth to examine their remains.

artisanal: describing something produced on a small scale, usually handmade by skilled craftspeople.

colony: a settlement in another country or place that is controlled by a "home" country.

commonwealth: an association of sovereign nations unified by common cultural, political, and economic interests and traits.

communism: a social and economic philosophy characterized by a classless society and the absence of private property.

continent: any of the seven large land masses that constitute most of the dry land on the surface of the earth.

cosmopolitan: worldly; showing the influence of many cultures.

culinary: relating to the kitchen, cookery, and style of eating.

cultivated: planted and harvested for food, as opposed to the growth of plants in the wild.

currency: a system of money.

demographics: the study of population trends.

denomination: a religious grouping within a faith that has its own organization.

dynasty: a ruling family that extends across generations, usually in an autocratic form of government, such as a monarchy.

ecosystems: environments where interdependent organisms live.

endemic: native, or not introduced, to a particular region, and not naturally found in other areas.

exile: absence from one's country or home, usually enforced by a government for political or religious reasons.

feudal: a system of economic, political, or social organization in which poor landholders are subservient to wealthy landlords; used mostly in relation to the Middle Ages.

globalization: the processes relating to increasing international exchange that have resulted in faster, easier connections across the world.

gross national product: the measure of all the products and services a country produces in a year.

heritage: tradition and history.

homogenization: the process of blending elements together, sometimes resulting in a less interesting mixture.

iconic: relating to something that has become an emblem or symbol.

idiom: the language particular to a community or class; usually refers to regular, "everyday" speech.

immigrants: people who move to and settle in a new country.

indigenous: originating in and naturally from a particular region or country.

industrialization: the process by which a country changes from a farming society to one that is based on industry and manufacturing.

SERIES GLOSSARY

integration: the process of opening up a place, community, or organization to all types of people.

kinship: web of social relationships that have a common origin derived from ancestors and family.

literacy rate: the percentage of people who can read and write.

matriarchal: of or relating to female leadership within a particular group or system.

migrant: a person who moves from one place to another, usually for reasons of employment or economic improvement.

militarized: warlike or military in character and thought.

missionary: one who goes on a journey to spread a religion.

monopoly: a situation where one company or state controls the market for an industry or product.

natural resources: naturally occurring materials, such as oil, coal, and gold, that can be used by people.

nomadic: describing a way of life in which people move, usually seasonally, from place to place in search of food, water, and pastureland.

nomadic: relating to people who have no fixed residence and move from place to place.

parliament: a body of government responsible for enacting laws.

patriarchal: of or relating to male leadership within a particular group or system.

patrilineal: relating to the relationship based on the father or the descendants through the male line.

polygamy: the practice of having more than one spouse.

provincial: belonging to a province or region outside of the main cities of a country.

racism: prejudice or animosity against people belonging to other races.

ritualize: to mark or perform with specific behaviors or observances.

sector: part or aspect of something, especially of a country's or region's economy.

secular: relating to worldly concerns; not religious.

societal: relating to the order, structure, or functioning of society or community.

socioeconomic: relating to social and economic factors, such as education and income, often used when discussing how classes, or levels of society, are formed.

statecraft: the ideas about and methods of running a government.

traditional: relating to something that is based on old historical ways of doing things.

urban sprawl: the uncontrolled expansion of urban areas away from the center of the city into remote, outlying areas.

urbanization: the increasing movement of people from rural areas to cities, usually in search of economic improvement, and the conditions resulting this migration.

INDEX

Italicized page numbers refer to illustrations.

INDEX

INDEX

INDEX

PHOTO CREDITS

COVER

ABOUT THE AUTHOR

Michael Centore is a writer and editor. He has helped produce many titles, including memoirs, cookbooks, and educational materials, among others, for a variety of publishers. He has experience in several facets of book production, from photo research to fact checking. His poetry and essays have appeared in *Crux*, *Tight*, *Mockingbird*, and other print- and web-based publications. Prior to his involvement in publishing, he worked as a stone mason, art handler, and housepainter. He was born in Hartford, Connecticut, and lives in Brooklyn, New York.